To

To is set in a pub somewhere owned by a savagely bickering together by the necessity of keeping the business During the course of the evening, a number of regular customers arrive and depart, events which trigger a fragile movement towards reconciliation between the couple.

Winner of the Manchester Evening News Best New Play award, **To** premièred at the Bolton Octagon in 1989 and opened at the Young Vic, London in November 1990.

Jim Cartwright lives in Lancashire, where he was born. **Road**, his first play, won *Drama* magazine's Best Play Award; the Samuel Beckett Award, 1986; was joint winner of the George Devine Award 1986 and *Plays and Players* Award, 1986. The TV version won the Golden Nymph Award for the best film at the Monte Carlo Television Festival. His other plays include: **Bed** (National Theatre, Cottesloe, 1989).

by the same author

Road
Bed

Jim Cartwright

To

METHUEN DRAMA

A Methuen Modern Play

First published in 1991 by Methuen Drama, Michelin House, 81 Fulham Road, London SW3 6RB and distributed in the United States of America by HEB Inc, 361 Hanover Street, Portsmouth, New Hampshire 03801.

Copyright © 1991 by Jim Cartwright

A CIP catalogue record for this book is available from the British Library

ISBN 0-413-63570-8

The photograph on the front cover is from the 1990 Young Vic production with Sue Johnston and John McArdle. Copyright © Gordon Rainsford. The photograph of the author on the back cover is copyright © Mark Gerson.

Permission has been given to reproduce the lines from *Are You Lonesome Tonight?* by Roy Turk and Lou Handman. © Redwood Music

Printed and bound in Great Britain by Cox & Wyman Ltd, Cardiff Road, Reading

Caution

To was first performed at the Bolton Octagon on 23 August 1989, with Sue Johnston and John McArdle playing all the characters:

Landlord
Landlady
Old Woman
Moth
Maudie
Old Man
Mrs Iger
Mr Iger
Lesley
Roy
Fred
Alice
Woman
Little Boy

Directed by Andrew Hay
Designed by Mick Bearwish
Lighting by Phil Clarke

Note

The action takes place over one night, in a pub, in the North of England.

To is designed so that two people can play all the characters. The set consists of a pub bar, with all glasses, pumps, till, optics etc., being mimed as are the other people in the pub to whom the actors relate. The costume changes should be kept to a minimum.

Blackness. Suddenly, lights up on **Landlord** *and* **Landlady** *behind bar working and serving.*

Landlord There you go love, two pints. Tar.

Landlady What was it now? Babycham and two Appletisers.

Landlord And now sir, a pint and a half of lager.

Landlady It was a Babycham wasn't it?

Landlord (*from mouth corner*) Get it together.

Landlady Sod off. (*To customer.*) There you go dear.

Landlord Thanks. And what's your poison? (*To someone else.*) Be with you in a minute.

Landlady Tar. Nice to see you two back together again. Yes.

Landlord (*while serving*) Er, can you see to this lad here love?

Landlady (*still to customer*) Right lovey, see ya. (*To* **Landlord**.) Eh?

Landlord Here love, customers, thirsty. (*Under breath.*) Move it woman.

Landlady Stuff it man. (*To customer.*) Yes love can I help you?

Landlord Right then, with ice was it?

Landlady Sorry, no cherries.

Landlord (*to* **Landlady**) What's them down there, blind arse.

Landlady You'll have a lager instead, okay. (*To* **Landlord**.) Don't get smart with me Pigoh.

Landlord Uh. There you go now. Thanks.

Landlady (*to someone leaving*) See you. What? Oooooooooh.

Landlord (*glares at her, then to customer*) Nice to see you, what's it to be? White wine and a Barbican.

Landlady Two double Drambuies, well well. Where the hell is that now?

Landlord There! There! (*Realises he's shouting and laughs back at customers. To* **Landlady**.) You'll be the death of me.

Landlady If only, if only.

Landlord Get damn serving.

Landlady I am. I am, if you'll keep your poxy nose out.

Landlord (*to customer*) Oh sorry. What was it again?

Landlady (*she cracks up laughing at this, he gives her a black look. To customer*) Two double Drambuies for you.

Landlord White wine and a Barbican. Not in the same glass I hope, ha!

Landlady (*at joke*) Oh my God. There you go loves. Tar.

Landlord Love, can you just reach me a Barbican from down there.

Landlady Where? Oh yes.

She crouches down for it. He quickly goes down too.

Landlady Ow.

Landlord (*comes up*) Here we are.

Landlady (*comes up, rubbing her side*) Little swine. Ow. I'll get you for that. (*To customer at bar.*) Yes. Ah it's the happy couple. What would you like then?

Landlord So that's four Grolshes, two Buds, and a packet of peanuts.

Landlady Two sweet white wines, how nice. You didn't get much of a tan then.

Landlord There you go, your wish is my command.

Landlady There you go, on the house.

Landlord *spins round to glare.*

Landlady Well it was this very pub in which you met, wasn't it? Yes. Lovely, lovely. See you later.

Landlord (*to* **Landlady**) On the house. Lovely. Lovely. (*Suddenly realises couple are waving to him from their table.*) What? Oh congratulations. Awww, our pleasure.

Landlady Creep.

Landlord Crap.

Landlady Fart.

Landlord Hag.

Landlady (*steps over to a customer*) Two whiskeys was it? (*And straight over his foot.*)

Landlord Arrr. Ohh.

Landlady Oh dear, are you all right, love? He wants to take the weight off his feet, I keep telling him. Now then, two whiskeys.

Landlord (*distracted by customer*) A brandy and cider, right you are. Not in the same glass I hope. Ha.

Landlady *cringes.*

Landlady (*taking money*) 2.05 loves. Tar now.

Landlord There's your brandy, we'll soon have the cider beside her.

Landlady Painful. Painful.

Landlord It will be. It will be.

Landlady Sorry? (*Turns towards customer's voice.*) Oh it's you, how are you? I was wondering when you'd pop up.

Landlord 2.50 thanks. Lovely. (*To* **Landlady** *as she passes.*) Don't embarrass us, you look like his grandmum.

Landlady Do you want what you had last night? Oooooooh, you young wag. No serious though, what's your choice love? Okay. Well thanks I will. Thanks very, very much, you gallant young boy.

Landlord A Southern Comfort and crisps. (*He goes to get them.*)

Landlady (*to* **Landlord***'s customer*) If he says 'Not in the same glass', don't laugh please.

Landlord Not in the same glass, I hope?

Landlady (*laughs, then to her customer*) Now then sparrow, there you go, and tar, tar again. (*She winks.*)

Landlord Get out and get some glasses while it's quietening. Go on.

Landlady I'm going. I'm a going. (*She does.*)

He breathes out. Grabs up a cloth and starts wiping glasses.

Landlord (*turns to audience*) First night in here? Well, you'll get used to us. We're a lively pub. It's calmed down a bit now, but it comes in waves. Not going to ask you what you're doing here, never do, that's one of our few rules. We get a lot of rendezvousers here you see, but we're also strong on couples, don't get me wrong. They either come in pairs or end up that way. That woman over there is my wife, bitch. I run this place virtually on my own. We've been here bloody years. In fact we met outside this pub when we were kids, me and cow. Too young to get in, snotty conked, on tip-toes peeking through the frosted windows. We had our first drink in here, we courted in here, we had our twenty first's in here, we had our wedding reception here, and now we own the bloody place. I only did it for her, it's what she'd always wanted. Done some knocking through recently, got the walls down, made it all into one. You can get around better, and more eyes can meet across a crowded room. Better that, better for business and pleasure and for keeping an eye on that roving tart. Where is she with them glasses? Wouldn't mind a bloody drink meself, I'll have one later. It's a constant battle keeping your throat away from the stock. It

really is the landlord's last temptation. Because this is it
for us proprietors. This is our life, these bar sides, to them
wall sides and that's it. People and pints and measures
and rolling out the bloody barrel. Working and social life
all mixtured, a cocktail you can't get away from. Until
night when we fall knackered to bed. But I'm not
complaining, no, no. As long as many mouths are clacking
at many glasses and the tills keep on a singing. What more
could a publican want?

Old Woman *enters*.

Landlord Oh here she is, I can set the clock by this auld
dear. (*Puts glass under pump ready*.) Evening love, usual?

Old Woman Yes please, landlord.

Landlord How's everything love?

Old Woman Passing same. Passing sames.

Landlord Oh aye. There you go.

Old Woman Thank you, landlord.

Landlord Pleasure lovey. (*He goes*.) Where is she with
them bloody glasses?

He exits. She sips her drink. Then turns to the audience.

Old Woman Here I am at the end of my day. Taking my
reward from the glass. He's at home, he can't come out,
too crippled dear. But he allows me out for my drink at the
end of it all, the day. I've retired, but not really, 'cause
now I have to work twice as hard with him, lifting his
shitty bum off the blankets. He's having all the last bit of
my life, but I don't begrudge him that. Poor lumped man
he is, there he is at home, with his pint of dandelion and
burdock, watching the television in the dark. All's I do is
look after him and shop a lot, shop a lot with nowt.

Though I do like to go shopping, I like to, I like the
butcher best, blood everywhere, laughing his bloody head
off. He's fat too, fat. Fat like jelly pork. Pink. I love him,
though he doesn't know of course. It's his laughing that
does it, and his big butcher life, chopping and pulling
those beasts apart. Admirable. Me, myself, don't have
much strength left now, carrying my husband down the
stairs, I have to stop three times, my arms keep giving.
'Let's have our breather' I say, and we both stop, panting
like knackered cattle. I watch his chest going like the
clappers, and I watch mine going the same. And all our
wheezes echoing off the stairway and my swollen ankles,
and his watery eyes, and I wonder in God's starry heavens
why we keep going. We have each other, we have the
allowance, there's a lot of memories somewhere, there's a
bit of comfort in sleep and Guinness, but what the hell has
it all been about? I ask you. I carry him down. I carry him
up, piss all over my hands. His day, the tele-box. My day,
shopping bag. Butchers for a bit o' scrag, see him flipping
open the animals with his very sharp knife. Oh my day,
my life, my day, my drink here. Him at home with the
tele, in the burdock dark a dead dandelion in his mouth. I
can hear his old chest creaking from here, and on my neck
his chicken arms, chicken arms, and around my neck his
poorly chicken arms. Get me a Guinness. Stand me a
drink. Fetch the butcher with his slaughtering kit, may I
ask you all to raise your cleavers now please and finish the
job, raise them for the bewildered and pig weary couples
that have stuck, stuck it out. Thank you.

She bows her head as though to have it cut off.

Lights pick up **Moth** *chatting a young woman up. Imaginary or
real from the audience.*

Moth You're beautiful you. You're absolutely beautiful
you. Look at you. You're fantastic you. I love you. I love

the bones of you. I do. You think it's too quick don't you.
But you can't see yourself. You're just . . . I'm in love with
you, I'm not joking. I've seen some women, but you. Let's
get back to what you are, beautiful. Did you just smile
then or did someone turn the lights on? You are beautiful
you. You stand for beauty. You sit for it too. Look how
you sit you, like a glamour model that's how. You
You're quiet though, but I love that in a girl, love that,
don't get me wrong. You're beauty you. Beauty itself.
Beauty is you. You're marvellous as well as being beautiful
too, you. Yes, too good for this place I'll tell you that.
What's a beautiful girl like you doing in a place like this,
or whatever they say, is that what they say, who cares,
who cares now, eh? You are a star, and you don't even
know it. A star before you start. Everything about you's,
just . . . You are it. The beauty of all times. You're just
beautiful and that's it! Done, finished, it. Because you are
the most beautiful thing ever brought to this earth. And
you're for me you. You are for me. There's no bones about
it, none! Here's the back of my hand, here, here. And
here's the pen, number, number please, number, before I
stop breathing.

Maudie *has entered and taps him on the shoulder.*

Maudie Hiyah Moth.

Moth What are you doing here?

Maudie I'm your bleeding bird aren't I?

Moth (*looking round*) Yes, yes, but . . .

Maudie Moth. Moth she wasn't interested.

Moth How do you know that?

Maudie Believe me I know. Moth, Moth do you still love
me?

Moth Of course I do, get them in.

Maudie No, I'm not this time.

Moth Eh?

Maudie I've had a good talking to by some of the girls at work today. And they've told me once and for all. I've not to let you keep using me.

Moth Using. Using. You sing and I'll dance. Ha! No Maudie you know that's not me. But when I'm broke what can I do, I depend on those that say they love me to care for me. And anyway it's always been our way.

Maudie Stop. Stop now. Don't keep turning me over with your tongue.

Moth Maudie, my Maudie.

He takes her in his arms, kisses her. She swoons.

Maudie Oh here get the drinks in.

Moth (*he opens handbag*) Ah that sweet click. (*Takes out some money.*) Here I go.

He sets off around the other side of bar to get served.

Maudie Oh no. No. Look he's off with my money again . . . I said this wouldn't happen again and here it is, happened. I've got to get me some strength. Where is it? (*Makes a fist and twists it.*) Ah there. Hold that Maudie. Maudie, Maudie hold that.

Moth *on his way back with the drinks. Bumps into someone. Dolly bird.*

Moth Oops sorry love. Bumpsadaisy. You all right . . .

Maudie Moth!

Moth See you. Better get these over to me sister. (*Passing others.*) 'Scuse me. (*Others.*) Yep yep. (*Others.*) Beep beep. Here we go Maud.

Maudie What were you . . . (*Shows fist to* **Moth**.)

Moth (*giving drink*) And here's your speciality.

Maudie Aww you always get it just right. Nobody gets it like you. The ice, the umbrella.

Moth Of course. Of course.

Maudie *kisses him.*

Maudie Oh look, I'm going again. All over you.

Moth That's all right, just watch the shirt.

They drink. He begins looking around. She looks at him looking around. She makes the fist again.

Maudie Look at me will you. Look at your eyes, they're everywhere, up every skirt, along every leg, round every bra rim. Why oh why do you keep chasing women!

Moth Oh we're not going to have to go through all this again are we petal. Is this the girls at work priming you?

Maudie Yes a bit, no a bit. I don't know. I can't remember now, so much has been said. I just want you to stop it.

Moth But you know I can't stop myself.

Maudie But you never even get off with them.

Moth I know.

Maudie It's like the girls say, I hold all the cards.

Moth How do you mean?

Maudie I'm the only woman on earth interested in you.

Moth Well yes, but . . .

Maudie Moth let it all go and let's get settled down.

Moth I can't it's something I've always done and I guess I always will. (*Again looking at some women.*)

Maudie No, Moth, no . . . Oh how can I get it through to you.

Moth (*draining his glass empty*) Drink by drink.

Maudie No way. Buzz off Moth.

Moth Come on love, get them in. Let's have a few and forget all this. You pay, I'll order.

Maudie No.

Moth But Maudie, my Maudie.

Maudie No, I'm stopping the tap. I shall not be used.

Moth Used. Used. Well if that's how you feel I can always go you know.

He walks down the bar a bit, stops, looks back, walks down the bar a bit, stops, looks back. Falls over a stool. Picks it up, laughs to cover embarrassment, limps back to her.

Maudie, I've been thinking, all what you're saying's so true and right as always. I'm losing everything, my flair, my waistline, what's next to go – you? Will it be you next?

Maudie (*unmoved*) You'll try anything won't you, just to get into my handbag. The romantic approach, the comic approach, the concern for me approach, the sympathy approach. Does it never end?

Moth You forgot sexy in there.

She swings for him, he ducks.

No Maudie. You're right again. What does a princess like you see in a loser like me?

Maudie I don't know. Well I do. You're romantic, like something on the fade. I love that.

Moth (*moving in*) Oh Maudie, my Maudie.

As he does, she starts to melt again, he starts to reach into her handbag, she suddenly sees this and slams it shut on his hand.

Maudie Stop!

Moth Aw Maud. How can I prove I'm genuine to you? Here take everything on me, everything, everything. (*Starts* *frantically emptying his pockets.*) My last 10p, I'm going to give it to you!

Maudie I don't want your poxy ten.

Moth You say that now, you say that now Maud, but you don't know what it's going to turn into. I'm going to give you all I've got left. My final, last and only possession. (*Spins and drops it in Juke box.*) My dancing talent.

'Kiss' by Tom Jones comes on. **Moth** *dances.*

Moth 'Cause Maud, whatever you say. Whatever's said and done. I'm still a top dancer 'ant I hey?

Maudie Well you can move.

Moth I can Maud. I sure as hell can Maud. (*Dancing.*) I'm dancing for you Maudie. For you only. (*Dancing.*) Come on get up here with me.

She comes to him, puts her handbag on the floor, they dance.

Moth Who's lost it all now eh?

He really grooves it.

Maudie (*worried, embarrassed*) Moth.

Moth Come on doll.

Maudie Moth take it easy.

Moth Come on. Swing it. Let your back bone slip. Yeah let your . . . Awwwwwwwa Ow ow!!! (*Stops. Can't move.*)

Maudie Moth, oh God, what is it?

Moth Me back, me back. Help oh help.

Maudie What can I do! What can I do!

Moth Get me a chair, get me a gin.

Maudie (*feeling up his back*) Where is it? Where is it?

Moth There between the whiskey and the vodka.

Maudie Ooo another trick, you snide, you emperor of snide! (*Hits him.*)

Moth No, no Maud. Really, you've got it all wrong. It's real. Arwwwwww. Get me to a chair!

Maudie It's real is it you swine?

Moth Real. Real.

Maudie Real is it?

Moth (*nodding*) Arrgh. Arrgh.

Maudie Okay let's test it.

Moth How?

She takes out a fiver and holds it in front of him. He tries to go for it, but he can't.

Maudie (*amazed*) It is true. (*Starts circling him.*) Trapped. At last after all these years, I finally have that fluttering Moth pinned down. Ha.

Moth Oh Maudie what you gonna do?

Maudie Let's see. Let's see here.

Moth Don't muck about now. I'm dying here, arrrgh, dying.

Maudie So if, if, I help, what do I get out of it?

Moth Anything! Anything!

Maudie Anything, anything eh?

Moth Yes, yes, arrrrgh.

Maudie Okay, make an honest woman of me now.

Moth No, never, arrrr.

Maudie Okay, see you love.

Moth No. Don't go Maud please.

Maudie Sorry love, have to, love to stay but . . . 'bye. And if any of you try to help him, you'll have me to deal with, and my handbag.

Maudie *blows him a kiss as she goes. Exits.*

Moth MAUD! Will you marry me?

Maudie (*coming back*) Sorry?

Moth Will you marry me?

Maudie YES! OH YESSSSSSSSS! (*She comes running to him and hugs him.*)

Moth (*she's hurt his back*) AARRRRGHHHH!

Maudie Oh sorry love.

Still in embrace she guides him to a stool.

Moth A a aa a.

She props him against stool and bar, he is stiff like a board.

Moth Ah.

Maudie Oh Oh. (*Cuddling him.*) Oh. (*Suddenly serious.*) Do you still mean it?

Moth I mean it. I mean it. Singleness is all over for me.

Maudie (*hugging him again as best she can*) Oh Moth you won't regret this.

Moth Arrgh. I know. I know.

Maudie I'll get us a taxi. Hold on now. Be brave. You poor thing.

She rushes out.

Moth (*turns to girl at front*) You're beautiful you. Look at you. You're fantastic you.

Blackout.

Landlady *enters from where they exited.*

Landlady (*calling back*) Handcuff him Maudie, handcuff him now. (*To audience.*) Look at that Maudie, over the moon and back, she wants to watch herself with that scallywag. Ahh, I enjoy a lull like this, you can get a decent chat in can't you? He hates lulls, if the till's not singing he starts crying. (*Waves to someone.*) All right. (*To someone else.*) Hiyah, I'll try and get over there in a minute. I like that part of pub life, the people. That's why it's a peach in here, so many people pairing up in front of your very eyes, very heart-warming, heart-rending. (*Looks off.*) Look at Pigoh go, the prat. (*Shouts.*) Hey you all right with those crates?

Landlord (*shouts from off*) Course I am. Bugger off!

Big crash is heard.

Landlady *titters.*

Landlord (*off*) OH MY GOD! MY PROFITS!

Landlady I don't know. Without me this place would collapse around the bastard, it really would. I'm the brains behind the operation you might say. He's got no idea really, he knows how to run around, but not how to run a pub. Sad but true, but funny too. You've got to laugh haven't you? This is our life, this public house and all who 'ale' in her. No social life, family life. Work, business, pleasure, all pulled from behind the bar, and beyond that only a loveless bed to lie in. Still, I have my consolations, like sipping away Pigoh's profits, and really, well there's never a dull moment when you deal in liquor. And you get to meet the choicest of people. Like this old love here.

Old Man *enters.*

Landlady How do Pops.

Old Man How do love.

Landlady What you on, a bitter or a stout?

Old Man Mild please.

Landlady Nothing like a change.

Old Man That's right dear.

Landlady You're a lovely old bugger you. Why don't you and me run away together. Just whisk me off me feet, I wouldn't say no.

Old Man Ha Ha.

Landlady Oh well, there you go Pops. (*Gives him drink.*) No, have it on me.

Old Man (*trying to pay*) Nay, here.

Landlady No, my treat.

Old Man Thank you.

Landlady My pleasure. (*Off to serve someone else.*) Yes love. (*Exits.*)

Old Man Howdo. (*Sups beer.*)

Pause.

They all think I'm quiet. (*Sups.*)

Long pause.

But there's a good reason for that.

Pause.

I'm having a very good time within.

Pause.

(*Smiles.*) With my wife. She's dead, but still with me. Not like a ghost or any of that old kak.

Pause.

It's just a feeling. (*Sups.*)

Don't go yet, I'm not mad tha' knows.

Pause.

Sometimes if the feeling's not come of its own
I can generally bring it on
by touching our teapot,
brown pot,
and this'll start something
brewing,
sweet,
present,
soft
as her cotton hair.

Long pause.

Then it deepens. (*Closes his eyes.*)

Pause.

She's here now.

Nice.

She was here when I came in
but it's more better now.

Pause.

It's like . . .

Pause.

Being held.

It's just

comfort of her
without anything else.

Pause.

She's gone now. (*Opens eyes.*) So that's how we come and go to each other during the day. (*Sups.*)

Pause.

And how deep we do soak in each other sometimes. So deep I can hardly stand from the chair. And this is how I think I'll go one day. I'll just tag on and slip off with her when she leaves. And somebody will come round to our house and find my empty shell. (*Chuckles, drinks, rests.*) Life's just passing in and out in't it? Very comfortable, very nice to know that. (*Finishes drink.*) Ta tar. (*Goes.*)

Landlady *enters with sandwich.*

Landlady Cheese and onion! (*To someone close by.*) Keep your eyes off, you. I've done this as a favour for . . . Where is she? (*Sees her, goes to her.*) There you are love, get that down you. (*Takes money.*) Tar. (*To someone else.*) Love the trousers, who'd have thought they'd come back in. Only joking love, very natty them.

Landlord *enters.*

Landlord The queen of tittle tattle.

Landlady Sod off.

Landlord Out of the cellar and into the boxing ring, that's me. (*Hits the bar side, enters bar.*)

Landlady (*also enters bar, puts money in till*) Ting ting, tills away, round bleedin' one.

Landlord Will you back off for once.

Landlady Never.

Landlord (*to customer*) Same again Jack? (*Puts glass up to optics.*)

Landlady (*to her customer*) Just the one pet, sure. (*She reaches up to optics, their arms cross.*)

Landlord What's up with you tonight?

Landlady I think you know.

Landlord (*gives drink, takes money*) Ta mate.

Landlady (*gives drink, takes money*) Thanks love.

They both come back to till and put money in.

Landlord I don't know what you're on about.

Landlady (*she closes till*) Ting ting, round two. Yes you do, yes you do.

Landlord Run a pub.

Landlady (*turns into corner to work*) That's it, turn to the ropes when the jabs get too close.

Landlord (*looks up*) What the bloody hell's this coming in!

Landlady Ting ting, match postponed!

Landlord It's a stag party. Man the pumps, pull out the stops, raise the prices, come on let's polish them off. You take the spirits, I'll take the beers.

Landlady *leaves without him noticing.*

Well then Gents, what's it to be? Five pints of lager, three bitter, two whiskeys one with ice, one without, gin, gin, gin and tonic. Treble tequila, Guinness, spritzer, brown and bitter, Barbican, Budweiser, Bloody Mary, Black Velvet and a Becks, Triple X, Tiopepe, Martini, vodka and shandy and a brandy, Pernod, peanuts, crisps, crisps, crisps, crisps, crisps, crisps, crisps, two rum and okey cokey colas, and a Cherry B and cider for the groom. We'll sort that for you lads, won't we dear, (*Turns to see she's gone.*) dear, *dear!* (*Hits the bar, exits.*)

Lights up on **Mrs Iger**, *arms folded, perched on bar stool nodding to the long scream and the opening strains of Led Zeppelin's 'Whole Lotta Love'. Music suddenly stops. She speaks.*

Mrs Iger I love big men. Big quiet strong men. That's all I want. I love to tend to them. I like to have grace and flurry round them. I like their temple arms and pillar legs and synagogue chests and big mouth and teeth and tongue like an elephant's ear. And big carved faces like a naturreal cliff side, and the Roman empire bone work. And you can really dig deep into 'em, can't you? And there's so much. Gargantuan man, like a Roman Empire, with a voice he hardly uses, but when he does it's all rumbling under his breast plate. So big, big hands, big everything. Like sleeping by a mountain side. Carved men. It's a thrill if you see them run, say for a bus, pounding up the pavement. Good big man, thick blood through tubular veins, squirting and washing him out. It must be like a bloody big red cavernous car wash in there, in him, and all his organs and bits hanging from the rib roof, getting a good daily drenching in this good red blood. They are so bloody big you think they'll never die, and that's another reason you want them. Bloody ox men, Hercules, Thor, Chuck Connors, come on, bring your heads down and take from my 'ickle hand. Let me groom and coddle you. And herd you. Yes, let me gather all you big men of our Isles and herd you up and lead you across America. You myth men. Myth men. Myth men. Big men love ya.

Little man approaches her.

Mr Iger Dear, I'm having difficulty getting to the bar again. Would you go?

Mrs Iger No. You get back in there and bring us drinks. Now.

Mr Iger I'll have another try shall I dear?

Mrs Iger No, not a try. Get them here. It's pathetic.

Mr Iger (*trying to get through the crowd*) 'Scuse . . . sorry . . .

Ow . . . Are you in the queue . . . Oh . . . Sorry . . . Could
I squeeze . . . ? No . . . Thanks . . . (*Suddenly wiping himself.*)
It's all right. It's all right. My fault . . . Whose turn is it,
do you know? . . . Well I only asked . . . Two please . . .
Hello . . . two . . . could I . . . 'scuse . . . Here love! Ah yes,
yes, could I . . . What? (*Leans back and looks up.*) Oh yes I
think you, perhaps, were first, that's right. Please go ahead
. . . Oh no, she's going to kill me. We've been in here an
hour and we've not drank yet. It's always the same. Dear,
deary me.

He suddenly notices two unattended drinks by him.

What about these two here. I couldn't. (*Looks about.*)
Could I?((*Looks about.*) I have to.

He slips off with them and back to her.

Mr Iger Here we go dear.

Mrs Iger At last. (*She takes a drink then splutters out.*) What's
this, we don't have alcoholic drinks.

Mr Iger I know, but that's all they had.

Mrs Iger You. Oh well, I'm not waiting another hour,
they'll have to do. But I must say, I must say, it is another
typical cock up by Mr Feeble man. I mean what's to
getting to a bar for a drink? Are you man or mouse?

He tries to speak.

Squeak, squeak, there's my answer. You should do
something about all this. I mean it's typical, too typical of
the little. I mean if you were big, big as I wanted, well,
well . . .

Mr Iger *suddenly cracks.*

Mr Iger (*crazed*) Right then drinks is it? Drinks. I can get
drinks. Right then. Here I go. I'm coming through. (*Barges
through to the bar.*) Straight through. I get them in, me.
Drinks. I'm the drink man. I was before everyone, me.

Everyone. (*To someone.*) Shut your face fatso. Come on now drinks, drinks, drinks for me, us, short ones, long ones . . .

As he continues raving, **Mrs Iger** *comes through.*

Mrs Iger Excuse me. Let me through. Thank you.

Mr Iger . . . I'll take all them orange ones, them green and them brown. Come on drinks here, come on, come on drinks . .

She hits him on the back of the head, he stops.

Mrs Iger Now what's to do?

Mr Iger Drinks you wanted. I was before everyone. Drinks I say.

Mrs Iger Calm.

Mr Iger I can get drinks. I can. Oh yes.

Mrs Iger Calm.

Mr Iger Drinks I will get, will.

Mrs Iger Calm.

Mr Iger Drinks.

Mrs Iger Calm.

He goes quiet.

Mrs Iger What is it?

He's quiet.
It's me, isn't it with just too much talk of the large.

He nods.

Ay dear, what have I done to you, my dinky.

Putting her arm around him.

Mr Iger Dinky?

Mrs Iger Yes. Come here my detailed little man.

She takes him in her arms.

Your weediness is welcome here.

They separate.

Come away now. Come on. My compact chap. (*Briskly.*)
We'll do something nice, take a walk, get some fresh air.

They exit. Offstage.

Mr Iger Dear?

Mrs Iger Yes?

Mr Iger Does this mean I can sleep in the bed tonight?

Mrs Iger Don't push it.

Landlord *enters holding a bottle high.*

Landlord Here it is. Last one ever. I knew I'd seen one in
the cellar. A bloody 'Bull's eye' brown. Look at that then.
(*He undoes it.*) There you go. (*Gives it to customer.*)

Landlady *comes in, begins serving someone as soon as she enters.*

Landlady Whiskey love? Yep. (*She turns to get it.*)

Landlord (*to* **Landlady**) Hey, look who's here having a
bloody 'Bull's eye' brown.

Landlady Smelly Jimmy. Well well. We've not seen you
for years.

She continues her job of filling glass with whiskey.

How are you?

Landlord
Landlady } (*in response*) Oh we're all right.

Landlady Well I am.

She turns to serve her customer. Then, in response to something Jimmy says:

Eh. (*She drops glass, it breaks. She can't speak.*) Don't you know?

Landlord (*quickly*) Hey Jimeny, come round here mate. This side here. Come on. (*Leads him off.*) You'll remember these lot of ugly mugs won't you? (*Offstage.*) Hey, look what the cat's brought in.

Landlady (*to her customer*) Sorry love.

Gets another whiskey for them. Takes money.

Tar. Tar.

Puts it in till.

Landlady *starts kicking glass under bar.*

Landlord *enters.*

Landlord Don't do that.

He gets down picking glass up.

Landlady Why? I thought you liked things shoved out of sight.

Landlord Don't know what you mean.

Landlady You do.

Landlord *turns away, starts doing something.*

Landlady Don't you think it's funny someone should say that, tonight of all nights. Don't you?

Landlord (*picking up empty bottle off bar*) Imagine finding a bloody 'Bull's eye' brown, eh?

Landlady Don't you?

Landlord I'll save that empty as a memento.

He puts it on shelf. She grabs it and shoves it in bin.

Landlady There's already two empty mementos behind this bar.

Landlord (*turning to serve someone*) Two pints sir. One lager, one bitter.

Landlady (*behind him, penetratingly*) Don't you think it funny though someone should ask . . . Don't you?

Landlord (*puts glass under lager tap*) Lager.

Landlady Don't you? Don't you?

Landlord (*worn down, puts glass under bitter tap*) Sorry, bitter's off. I'll just go and see to that. (*Goes quickly.*)

Landlady *lifts glass of lager, gives to customer. Tries bitter tap. Laughs.*

Landlady He was wrong again. I thought as much. Look at that. Bitter's never off here dear. (*Filling glass. Looking after* **Landlord**.) Never.

Interval – if required.

Landlord *enters collecting glasses.*

Landlord Busy now, eh? You can see it busy now, eh? The hectic hour. There's been a lot of copping offs round that side, two fallings out here, and a fight, three proposals of marriage round there, and a birth in the snug. And it's nowhere near last orders yet! Not really. Not really. I always say that about this time. I like a crack with the customers now and again. Better than a crack from them, eh? Eh? So you're still here then. Glad to see it. Keep drinking that's my motto, don't stop till you drop, that's my other. Glass harvesting time now. Collect 'em in.

Collect 'em in, wish they'd bring their own. Come on, sip, swig, and sup (*Under breath.*) ya buggers. That's right. All right if I take your glasses love. Not the ones you're wearing. No put them back. (*Turns to audience.*) Bloody hell.

Landlord *crosses to woman,* **Lesley,** *sitting on her own.*

Landlord Hello love, where is he tonight then?

Lesley *mumbles something.*

Landlord Hey?

Lesley *mumbles again.*

Landlord At bar?

Lesley Yeah.

Landlord (*looks round*) Looks like you've lost him then. You'll never find him again in all that lot. Look at 'em all. Lovely thirsty boozers. My favourites. Better get her back and serving. (*Looks off.*) Look at her entertaining the rabble.

Landlord *goes.*

Lesley *looks around, then looks down. Looks around, then looks down.*

Roy *comes over with drinks.*

Roy What were he on about?

Lesley Nowt, he were just collecting glasses.

Roy Oh. Here you are. (*Puts drinks down. Sits.*) She's a character that landlady.

Lesley She is.

They drink. Pause.

Lesley What you on?

Roy Mild.

She nods. They sit in silence.

Roy There's more strange things happen in a pub than there do on T.V. Eh?

Lesley Aye. Could I just . . . ?

Roy Bloody hell, what did your last slave die of? Bloody Hell! I've only just sat down.

Lesley No. I wanted to know if I could go to loo.

Roy 'Course you can. Okay go.

She stands up.

But don't be long.

She begins to move.

Hey, and look down.

Lesley Eh?

Roy Keep your eyes down. Every time you look up, you look at men you.

Lesley I don't.

Roy (*pointing at her*) Eh, hey, no back chat. (*Looks quickly around, making sure no one's heard him.*) Go on.

She goes.

Roy (*to someone*) Mike.

Pause.

(*To someone else.*) Sandy.

Pause.

She comes back and sits.

Roy What did you have?

Lesley Eh?

Roy What did you have, one or two?

Lesley One.

Roy You were a long time for a one.

Lesley There was someone in as well.

Roy Christ, I s'pose you got chatting.

Lesley No.

Roy No.

Lesley No.

Roy Don't 'no' me.

She edges back.

Did you say 'owt about me?

Lesley No.

Roy Who did you talk about then, someone else?

Lesley No.

Roy I told you with your no's. Who did you talk about?

Lesley We didn't even talk.

Roy Didn't even talk. Don't gi' me that. Two women in a woman's shithouse and they don't speak. You must think I'm soft. Do you?

Lesley What?

Roy Think I'm soft.

Lesley I don't know.

Roy What do you mean, don't know?

Lesley Well, I can't say no you said.

Roy Oh, if I said put your hand in the fire would you? Would you?

She shakes her head.

Roy Why not?

She looks away.

Roy No but you can talk about men in women's toilets can't you love, eh?

She keeps looking away.

If you don't answer, that means yes.

Lesley No.

Roy If you say no, two things happen: one I know you're lying, two I think about hittin' you in the face.

Lesley *looks down. He nods to someone across bar.*

Roy So, do you wanna stay here or move on?

Lesley Mmm.

Roy Christ I don't know why I bother. You've no conversation have you? Have you?

Lesley Mmm.

Roy See what I'm on about. I might as well go out with a piece of shit from that favourite woman's bog of yours, where you spent all our night.

Pause.

Do you want some more crisps?

Lesley Mmm.

Roy Well liven up then and you might get some later on. What about some 'Wotsits'?

Lesley Yes.

Roy Well there you are then. Liven up and you might get some 'Wotsits'.

Pause.

Roy They've done a nice job in here 'ant they, eh? He did a lot of it himself, knocked the snug out and everything. What's over there?

Lesley Eh?

Roy What's over there so interesting?

Lesley Nothing, I just moved me head I . . .

Roy I see. Watching the darts were you? Eh?

Lesley No I . . .

Roy What?

Lesley I don't know.

Roy Don't know. I do. See that little git in the jeans and shirt, there, him.

She looks.

Roy Okay you've seen enough now. Well I could break him like that, with my knee and my arms. Break the little wanker like that. Okay? Okay?

Lesley Okay.

Roy Would you be sad?

Lesley I don't know. I don't even know him.

Roy But you'd like to wouldn't you?

Lesley No.

Roy No. Are you sure?

She nods her head.

Roy It's just that 'okay' sounded a bit sad.

Lesley What 'okay'?

Roy That 'okay' you said before sounded a bit sad. After I'd said I'd break the little wanker. That one.

Lesley (*confused*) Oh.

Roy *stares at her a long time.*

Roy Don't make me feel small.

Lesley I'm not.

Roy I'm not having you or him or anyone making me feel small.

Lesley I'm not.

Roy Well, I just said all that then, and then felt small.

Lesley What?

Roy About him and you, and that 'okay', and you made me feel small after. When it was your fault, I said it in the first place, for looking at him.

Lesley (*beaten*) Oh.

Roy Well.

Lesley What?

Roy Are you not going to say sorry?

Lesley Sorry.

Roy Right. (*To someone across bar, raises his glass.*) Aye get 'em down yeah. Ha.

Silence.

Roy You've gone quiet. What you thinking of?

Lesley Nothing.

Roy No, no. Hold on. No. Who you thinking of?

Lesley (*pleading*) Oh Roy.

Roy No, no. When someone's quiet they're thinking, right?

Lesley Maybe.

Roy Maybe. That's a funny word to say, maybe. What you saying maybe for? That means you were. Who?

Lesley I wasn't.

Roy Who? If you wasn't, you would have said no. Who were you thinking of?

Lesley No one.

Roy Who? (*Waits.*) Who?

She shakes her head.

Roy Hey, remember what I said about no. Who?

She looks down.

Who?

She looks down more.

Who?

Lesley (*suddenly jumps up*) No one. No one at all. Can't I even have me own mind!

Roy (*embarrassed*) Sit down. Sit down.

Lesley I can't win. If I said I was thinking of every man in here naked, or I said I was thinking of you and the baby, it wouldn't make any difference. You'd still find a way of torturing me wouldn't you? Torturing! Torturing!

She storms out.

He looks round grinning, embarrassed.

Pause.

She comes back in.

Lesley I need the front door key.

Roy (*gently*) Hey, sit down love. Please sit.

She still stands.

I'm sorry. I realise what I must have done to you now. I don't know what it is. It's 'cause I care like. You know. I get carried away. Come on, sit down, please.

She does.

(*Soft.*) I didn't expect you to do that love.

Suddenly slaps her.

(*Vicious.*) You'll never do it again.

Instant blackout.

Landlord *going behind bar.*

Landlord Winding down now, winding down. We're over the top of the hill and half way down the other side. In other words the mad rush is over. So . . . (*Reaches for a glass, puts it under optics.*) Should I? Shouldn't I? Should I? Shouldn't I? Or . . . (*Puts glass under pumps.*) Should I? Shouldn't I? Should I? Or . . .

Landlady *walks in and goes straight to optics, puts her glass under. Lets measure one, two, three come out. He is watching agape. She goes and lounges against bar.*

Landlord What's going on?

Landlady Where?

Landlord Here. With your (*Mimics action.*) one, two, three. We don't do all this for nothing you know.

Landlady Ah, sod off.

Landlord How many have you had tonight anyway?

Landlady Three dray men, five regulars, a few lager louts, and the 'Cheesies' rep.

Landlord It wouldn't surprise me. It would not surprise me.

She lifts her glass in a cheers.

Landlord Come on how much? Let me smell your breath. Let me.

He goes up to her face, she turns away, he sniffs.

Landlady Don't get too close, we might accidentally kiss.

Landlord You're half sozzled, aren't you?

Landlady I'd say more than half actually.

Landlord Bloody great in'it. Bloody great.

Landlady Oh shut up.

He suddenly grabs glass off her and throws its contents down the sink. She's angry at first. Then just lounges back. Laughs.

Landlord I'd rather do that, than you have it.

Landlady Oh.

Landlord (*still looking down sink*) Yes, I would.

Landlady Oh I bet it hurt that, like throwing your blood away.

Landlord You just don't care any more do you? It may have escaped your notice, but we're trying to make a living here.

Landlady (*picking up a glass again*) This helps me to keep living here.

She goes toward optics with it. He puts his hand on hers to stop her.

Landlady Get off.

Landlord No.

Landlady Get off or I'll scream like I've been stabbed.

Landlord Do it then.

She begins to open her mouth. He lets her go. She goes to optic, gets another drink.

Landlord I'm going, I can't watch this.

Landlady What, me drinking, or your precious profits on the drip?

Landlord *doesn't look at her. He just leaves.*

She goes to drink. But can't now. Puts it down. Puts her hand over her eyes.

Blackout.

Lights up.

Fred *enters and sits.* **Alice** *enters, eating crisps, turns T.V. on, sits beside him.*

Fred Well, shall we get a drink in?

Alice I wouldn't mind so much.

Fred Well, get them in then.

Alice I will after this next programme.

Fred Okay.

Silence. She starts looking round.

Fred What you doing?

Alice I'm just looking round.

Fred You're doing counting things again.

Alice I'm not.

Fred You damn are. Do you want to go back in that white place wid' the closed doors?

Alice No fear, no.

Fred Well hang onto yourself then.

Alice I've never been the same since Elvis died.

Fred You killed him.

Alice How?

Fred By buying his records which gave him money for drugs which killed him.

Alice The King never took drugs.

Fred Not freaky drugs but slimming pills and all that, dried his blood up, constipated him. Choked his bum, he died of a choked bum.

Alice Such kingliness gone.

Fred You're fat and old.

Alice You're exactly the same.

She looks at the T.V.

Alice He's exactly the same as well.

Fred Who?

Alice Him there, behind Kirk Douglas. Very Fat.

Fred He is too. He's not going to get on that palomino horse is he?

Alice No way.

Fred He bloody is you know. You just watch.

They watch.

Alice No, they've both gone out the picture now.

Fred Do you think that's it with them now?

Alice Probably.

Fred I hope the horse comes back towards the end.

Alice It won't.

Fred What a swizz.

Silence.

Fred If I was at home I'd turn the bloody thing off.

Alice I know you would, that's why we came to the pub.

Fred Well it's not to drink that's for sure. I've only had two.

Alice Well you'll have to hang on till we're both ready.

Fred I'm ready now.

Alice Well I nearly am.

Silence.

Fred Well, what we waiting for, the film or the crisps?

Alice All the lot.

She finishes crisps: tips the packet and drains it. While he's not looking, she blows it up and pops it in his ear. They look round and start laughing.

Fred Oh ha, I don't know.

Alice Hee hee.

Fred Ha.

Suddenly points at television screen.

Fred There's the palomino again. Look at him go!

Alice I don't believe it, and the fat man too. They've gone now.

Fred I recognised him then. He was in the background in some other film we watched.

Alice I wonder if we'll see him in something else.

Fred Let's remember him, we'll give him a name.

Alice What?

Fred 'Fat-Fat'.

Alice 'Fat-Fat' what?

Fred 'Fat-Fat Palomino'.

Alice 'Fat-Fat Palomino' our favourite star.

Fred He's probably dead now, these are old pictures.

Alice Aw, I hope not.

Fred Oh, don't have the water works.

Alice I'm not. I'm not that sad about him.

Fred He was a bloody good extra though.

Alice He was.

Fred I wouldn't mind trying that.

Alice You're too fat and old.

Fred He was fat and old.

Alice Yeah, but he was a different fat and old.

Fred What do you mean?

Alice He was American-Ranch-style fat and old.

Fred What's that mean?

Alice There's different fat and olds all over the world.

Fred And what fat and old am I? English fat and old?

Alice No, sad fat, poor old.

Fred Well now I know. Anyway, you're just fat and old. Fat and old all over your little chair.

Alice We're middle-aged anyway.

Fred I know, but we look old with our fat.

They both watch tele awhile. The film ends.

Fred It's finished. Turn the tele off.

Alice Why?

Fred We turned it on.

Alice You do it.

Fred I can't with my legs.

She does. She comes back and sits.

Alice (*sings*) Are you lonesome tonight?

Fred So get them in now.

Alice (*sings*) Do you miss me tonight?

Fred Shall we get them in now?

Alice (*sings*) Are you sorry we drifted apart? (*Goes silent.*)

Fred You've gone again haven't you?

Alice It's me nerves, I can't help it.

Fred Come on, let's go home and play records.

Alice I'll cry.

Fred I'll dabble your tears.

Alice We're close in our way.

Fred Close as we can get with our fat.

Alice We've been unlucky in life but luckyish in love.

Fred Yes.

Alice Will you call me Priscilla tonight?

Fred Yes I will. (*Pause.*) Will you call me 'Fat-Fat Palomino'?

They leave. Blackout.

Landlord *enters.*

LAST ORDERS NOW. COME ON. COME ON. LAST ORDERS. LAST. LADIES AND GENTS.

Begins collecting glasses.

(*To someone in audience.*) He's had a few too many an't he love? Look at that, eh. You wanna get him home. Do you know the fireman's lift?

Last orders everybody. We've reached the point of no
return. Last orders now. Come on slow throats. Last
orders at the bar.

(*To someone leaving.*) Goodnight. Take care now.

(*To someone as he collects lots of glasses up.*) Did you drink all
them yourself Missus? Bloody hell, you can come again
you can.

He stacks them on the bar.

Any more for any more?

Last orders.

Exits.

A **Woman** *enters, slightly drunk.*

Woman (*to audience*) Are they still serving? I mustn't leave
this corner for the moment. I'm the 'Other Woman', come
where she shouldn't to look at my man. My man and his
wife. I've not come incognito either. I've come as my
bloody self, drinky, smart, a little crumpled, used to being
dressed up at the wrong time in the wrong places. In the
only car on a car park after dark. In strange houses in the
afternoon. At bus stops in last night's make-up. And I'm
not having it no, no more Mister. (*She takes out a fag,
fumbles with it, drops it.*) I've come here tonight, so he can
see us both. Not one in one world and one in another, but
both under the same light and choose. (*As in a child's
choosing rhyme.*) Ip, dip, ip, dip, ip, dip. You see this is the
last time I'm going to love. I haven't got it in me to go
again. So it's to be him, or it's to be something else, but
not another man. No, no more. Where's that fagarette?
Did I drop it? Toots to it, toots to the lot of it. Did he look
then? (*She tugs at her scarf, it falls.*) He did, I'm sure. Oh
Jesu! Jesu! I want him. I want to wave and scream. She

doesn't know, you know. I can tell, see, see that laugh she makes, too free, too free by far. I think. That's how it is in flick and shadow land, it's all thinking of others and their movements and I am sick to the soul with it. What will he do? What will she say? Will he come? Will he cancel? Is that the door? Was that the car? Dare I shower? Will he ring? Most times these wives, you know, they don't even want them. They won't have love with them, you know. They put them down, you know. But they won't let them loose. My God, they will not let them loosey. And I love loosey. Oh my God, he's coming over. Face him, face him. No shift, shift, shift. Face him. Shift. (*She turns away.*)

Out of the dark the **Landlord** *approaches, collecting glasses. She turns, they come face to face. Pause.*

Where is he?

Landlord Who, love?

Woman A man and his woman, they were coming this way.

Landlord They just passed you love, and went out.

Woman Follow that couple.

She rushes after them.

Landlady (*from offstage*) Watch out love, you nearly had me over.

Landlady Who was that?

Landlord She left her scarf.

Landlady Well, take it after her quick unless you want to wear it.

Landlord *takes it and exits.*

Landlady *starts to put a few bottles, glasses away.*

Landlady (*to someone leaving*) Goodnight. Yeah, see you. You do if you dare. Tara. (*To someone else.*) One for the road is it? Okey doke. There you go love, thanks. (*To someone at door.*) Night.

She turns back and starts: a little boy is there.

Boy Is me Dad here?

Landlady What do you say lovey?

Boy Is me Dad here?

Landlady Well I don't know love, do you want to hitch up here and see if you can see him?

Boy *nods.* **Landlady** *lifts him up on counter.*

Landlady Can you see him?

Boy *shakes his head.*

Landlady What's his name?

Boy Frank.

Landlady Is it Frank Leigh?

Boy *nods.*

Landlady Oh, he's gone love, he left a while ago.

Boy *nods at her words, and then starts crying his eyes out.*

Landlady Oh dear, come on love, don't cry, eh?

Boy I want my Dad.

Landlady I know you do love. I know. Where've you been?

Boy (*in sobs*) He left me outside with some pop and some crisps and he's forgot me.

He starts crying again.

Landlady (*loving him*) Now, now, eh.

Boy I want my Dad.

Landlady Don't worry love, he'll be back. Listen now, listen. Is your Mummy at home?

Boy No, she's in hospital.

Landlady Well, I'll tell you what, if he doesn't turn up soon we'll go and find him, shall we? How's that, eh?

He seems to have calmed now. Then he suddenly starts crying again.

Landlady It's all right love. Hey, hey, come on now. I'll tell you what, let's have some more crisps shall we, while we're waiting eh?

He nods.

Landlady Okay. (*She goes behind bar.*) Let's see what we've got here. (*Suddenly she looks over and beyond him.*) Now look who I can see. Look who's just come back. (*Looking towards door.*)

Boy (*looks*) DAD! (*Tries to jump off, can't.*)

Landlady *helps him down, he almost starts to belt off.*

Landlady Hey, hey. You forgot something.

Gives him crisps. Then holds his face between her hands and kisses his forehead, lingering, looking at him, the child looking back. Then suddenly she comes round.

Go on now. Off you go.

He runs out towards his Dad. She watches him go. Then goes behind the bar. Gets a drink.

Landlord (*enters, calling back*) Hey Frank, what have I told you about kids in here? I don't know.

(*To customers.*) All right, could you drink up now. Tar. (*To* **Landlady**.) Drop the towel over the taps love.

She just turns away.

(*He takes another glass.*) Tar. (*Holds it up to look, turns it upside down, truly empty.*) You enjoyed that one didn't you. Bloody hell. Okay, see you. 'Night. Can we have your glasses please. Thank you. Tar. See you. Sleep tight.

Landlady 'Bye love.

Landlord Well that's that then. Another one over. Will you bolt up? What's up with you? Oh, I'll do it.

He goes off, hear bolts going.

He comes back in.

Landlord Come on then. (*He starts to get stuck in with the glasses.*)

Landlady Did you see that little boy?

Landlord Yeah I saw him. (*Still working.*)

Landlady Do you know what day it is today?

Landlord Yeah, another working one. Come on, let's get these lot away.

Landlady Okay. (*She puts her arm on top of counter and walks forward, all the glasses smashing to floor.*)

Landlord What you doing? OH CHRIST!

They stare at each other.

Landlady Shall I clear that side now?

She goes to do it. He grabs her.

Landlady Go on, hit me. But hit me hard.

Landlord *lets her go. He returns to work.*

Landlord I know what day it is.

Landlady Eh?

Landlord I said, I know what day it is. What do you think I am, stone?

He stops working. Looks down sink like he's going to be sick.

Landlady Seems that way.

Landlord *grabs a glass, goes to optic, lets two measures out.*

Landlady Don't.

Landlord Why not? You do.

Landlady I can stop. Oh go on, what's it to me.

Landlord That's more like it. That's nearer to it. I was getting a bit worried there, sounded like care. (*Drinks. Carries on working.*) Come on.

Landlady Eh?

Landlord Let's get going.

Landlady Is that it then? That's how you think it can go again. One little explosion, two little explosions, have a drink, carry on.

Landlord Huh. (*Working.*)

Landlady That's what's been going on for years and years. Every time we try to talk about it.

Landlord I don't know what you're on about.

Landlady You do.

Landlord Look, another time eh?

Landlady No. Not this night you don't. No slipping away. I want to talk about things.

Landlord Well I don't, okay?

Landlady You're a bastard. How the hell am I going to get this out then? How the hell am I going to get it out? I've no one to love it out of me, I've no one to knock it out of me. Just a blank man.

Landlord Tough.

She starts randomly knocking glasses off.

Landlord Don't hurt my pub!

She starts laughing.

Landlady It's not a person you know.

Landlord I know. But that's the sorry state of it. It's all I've got to care for.

Landlady Oh dear.

Landlord I hate you.

Landlady I hate you harder.

Landlord If that's the case, in these few precious hours we have to ourselves, why do we have to waste them on each other?

Landlady Because seven years ago tonight our son died . . .

There's a knock at the door. He goes out to it.

Landlord (*offstage*) No we're closed. No, no take away. No.

Bolts again. Comes back in. Continues clearing away.

Landlady I feel sick. That's the first time I've said that for almost as many years. Why did it sound corny on my lips? (*Looks up, he's not listening.*) You're not listening.

Landlord Well. (*Pause, cleaning.*) You've got to carry on. (*Pause, cleaning.*) You know that as well as I do.

She suddenly screams long, chilling and loud.

He turns to look at her, doesn't go to her, just watches until she's finished.

Then she looks up at him, like a shot animal.

Landlady I can't stand it no more! The blame hurts and burns too much.

Landlord I never blamed you.

Landlady Liar.

Landlord I did not blame you, all right?

Landlady Who did you blame then, yourself?

Landlord No.

Landlady Who did you blame then, him?

Landlord Don't say things like that!

Landlady What, leave him out of this, like he never existed, is that what you're saying?

Landlord Stop. Stop with your filth!

Landlady What? . . . You're mad.

Landlord (*back to work*) Leave the dead.

Landlady God you're worse than me.

Landlord (*working on*) I'm worse than no one, just leave it, eh?

Landlady Look we've got to get this out for our own sanity.

Landlord You worry about that, I'm all right.

Landlady It's rotted us.

Landlord Well, what's the point of bothering then?

Landlady You cold gone bastard.

Landlord Aye.

She grabs up a glass to him. He turns to her, lifts his chin.

Landlord Go on break it and shove it in where it's soft. Go on. (*Waits.*) You want to, and I don't mind.

She drops glass.

Landlady What have we come to?

She turns away.

He stays in that position, chin up.

Pause.

She turns back. She looks at him standing there like that.

Still in that position, like a statue, he speaks. Eyes closed.

Landlord I loved it when we all loved. When we all were
loving. Him and . . . When we were . . . Me and you
bickered like we do now, all very funny, all on the surface,
but love was underneath then. Now it's hate. Hate for
sure.

Silence.

Landlord *opens eyes.*

I see him every day.
My son.

Pause.

I remember when he could . . .
Pulling at the crates like his Dad.
He thought he could do it, didn't he?

I see him here like as . . .

In his pyjamas.

At night his hair was always . . . (*Touches his own head.*)
Peeping in the pub. You'd shout, but I'd always let him
in, and lift him up and on the counter.

Oh God, how do you die when you're seven years old.

Covers his eyes.

Pause.

When it happened I had to turn away. I thought later I
could turn back, but I couldn't. Nothing healed, it just
went harder and harder and harder.

Landlady And you blamed.

Landlord No.

Landlady Liar!

Landlord No.

Landlady A blaming man. A stupid blaming man.

Landlord No.

Landlady Yes!

Landlord You were driving!

Landlady Yes!

Landlord Let's stop this.

Landlady You can't do that to me. It has to be out!

Landlord No more. (*Shakes his head.*)

Landlady Yes, all of it. We were flung. Cars in the back
and side. And a over and a over. I looked at him, he was
going like a rag doll, this way and that, this way and that,
his little mouth wide open. Then I was gone. In the
ambulance, bits I remember, some blanket round me,
blood in the wool. At the hospital I remember nothing,
just a black, red, black, red, like some old coal, coming
and going for a very long time. When I came to I knew
he'd gone. Later, one of the nurses told me. Later, you
came. There were flowers everywhere. You told me you'd
buried him, you said you couldn't keep his body all that
time while I was in the coma. But I knew you'd done it
because you blamed me.

Landlord No.

Landlady He went without my goodbye. I didn't see him
in his suit and tie, in his little coffin. I saw him with his
mouth wide open.

Landlord Stop.

Landlady No. No. I couldn't tell what was left between us
in the hospital. But when I came home the cold set in.
Really frightening cold. And we stood like strangers
upstairs. And we've stood that way ever since.

He nods.

Pause.

Silence.

Landlord Please know now, I didn't blame you. And I didn't want to do that to you. But I couldn't touch anything. Please know. I had no blame. Just hard, everything hard.

Landlady Why couldn't you tell me that?

Landlord Couldn't say any . . . And from then on. All this time wouldn't talk about it, so you couldn't talk about it. I thought about it, but knew you thought I didn't. And in my quiet you thought I blamed, but I didn't. Such a lot of hurt inside. Solid. Hard.

Landlady We've held ourselves for all these years, sick of our own arms squeezing, squeezing.

They look at each other. It seems they're going to embrace. But he turns and takes a glass, and begins washing it.

Landlord In the morning, you bring his picture down and you put it up there, will you?

She nods.

They both start to clean up and put away a while, in silence.

Landlady I'll cash up tomorrow.

Landlord Aye. I'll just switch off.

He turns lights out.

In the dark.

Landlord I love you.

Landlady I love you too.

*Further titles in the
Methuen Modern Plays series
are listed overleaf.*